Staying at Nan's

Written by Charlotte Middleton

Illustrated by Lisa Smith

Every Friday, I stay at Nan's.

3

Nan gets up early.

I get up early, too.

We go for a ride.

7

Nan loves the park.

She plays on the swings.

8

I play, too.

q

Then we go swimming.

11

Nan loves swimming.

She is **very** good at swimming.

Nan was a champion swimmer.

Swimmer wins gold!

I want to be a champion, too.

Swimmer wins gold!

I love staying at Nan's.